RISING WITH A DISTANT DAWN

David Groulx

BookLand press

TORONTO, CANADA

Published by BookLand Press
6021 Yonge Street, Suite 1010, Toronto, Ontario, Canada M2M 3W2
www.booklandpress.com

Printed and bound in Canada.

Library and Archives Canada Cataloguing in Publication

Groulx, David, 1969-
Rising with a distant dawn / David Groulx.

Poems.
ISBN 978-1-926956-05-3

I. Title.

PS8563.R76R57 2011 C811'.54 C2011-905730-1

MIX
Paper from responsible sources
FSC® C004071

ANCIENT FOREST™ FRIENDLY

We acknowledge the support of the Canada Council for the Arts which last year invested $20.1 million in writing and publishing throughout Canada.
Nous remercions de son soutien le Conseil des Arts du Canada, qui a investi 20,1 millions de dollars l'an dernier dans les lettres et l'édition à travers le Canada.

Canada Council for the Arts Conseil des Arts du Canada

TABLE OF CONTENTS

THE WOMEN MOVED AWAY

The reserve was emptied
the women that had been there
moved away
with their children
in the back seats of old
Indian cars
it reminded me of *the grapes of wrath*
migrating to the city
just like okies/brown
and just like them
we bury the dead
along the roads
and just like them
in the women
lives the nation

I GREW UP WITH SOME STORIES

Stories my dad told me about
Albert Johnson, *the mad trapper of Rat River*
Kit Carson
my dad and Kit Carson
I sat on his knee while he drank beer
listening about Kit Carson, *friend of the Indians*
burning them out of house and home
stories of his brother and his horses
killed in Holland
my dad
who took my mother into town *like she was white*
he never spoke to me about the mine
the mine was silent
we were silent
heavy *like granite*

NATIVE CHILDREN HUFFING

I watch the children go to waste
suck life
out of a plastic bag of glue
death inhaled

they laugh
stagger
carry already dead
brothers and sisters

peel back memories
from their bones
and comb ashes
into black widow hair

COYOTE WATCHES THE WOMAN'S HEALING SONG

She sings
to our ancestors
while she cuts cedars
falling her boughs
making medicine
for the body
and
healing
for the soul

THE FORGOTTEN MAN

I woke up from beneath
the loading docks from
behind the liquor store
there was an old Indian there
wearing a green Canadian army jacket
drinking Aqua Velva
I gave him a bottle of Wiser's whiskey
he gave me his jacket
with his corporal stripes
I left him alone
with his bottle
to catch concrete beaches
and heal his aching memories

VOICES LOW/ON THE WINGS

With violence
the settler knows
how to terrorize
they burnt down
my brother's revolt
before I became
voices low/on the wings
before we were even born

FIRE

My mother is coming to light the fire
my mother is coming to light the fire
she is building
the four directions

in the centre
in the centre

she lights the fire
we are coming to eat
we are coming to eat
the fire is lit

WITH WHAT IS WASTED

I watch the kids
and see their mothers on their faces
worn/out and been
a history written flesh
an ink that bleeds
onto blank pages
and bleeds into their bodies
poor/broken and full of rage
soaking in this hurricane poverty
busted appliances
choking shacks
and abandon cars
row along dirt roads
dogs running loose
in packs
children running
in gangs

WHAT IS HIDDEN

I want to run back to the world
and kill the ghosts that haunt me now

I want to run back/past the shovel and plow
and touch the salt on the other side

I want to drink between these broken mountains
and touch again the earth

DISTANCE

There is a distance between you and me
and I want it to get longer and longer
I need this to grow
until I am free from the fire

further and further I go
carrying this broken mountain
I am walking/ running/ crawling
disappearing into the blue

drowning in this distance
I am defiant
waves of time smash into my body
between us they pile up the horizons

WALK/THIS GARDEN

This poem walks
this garden
wind wanders
blue moon rising
wild moon pursuing
molesting
a rancid corpse
earth eaten
wasted
death/ death blow
half to death
the live falling
failing to find peace
this poem walks

POETRY

It must be butchered
hands bare
wild wind
holy
skin torn off
flesh eaten raw
bones broken
red with rain
skeletons
dying
naked
this cannibalism
that creates
this life

CORPSE OF THE FROZEN WATER

The sharks wait for it
to melt
goading the corpse
circling to free it
hoping to eat it
to incinerate it
while it slowly drifts
to memory
clotted blood
encased in ice

A REOCCURRING ORDER

When the eagle kills the bull
and the condor rips all flesh from its bones
silent dead will'er our body
the moon will dance again
in fifty/yr/cycles

KNOWLEDGE OF EONS

The rope speaks
in knots
it punishes
the poor
the wheel knows
mysteries
it is silent to
the deaf
they move
memory
to mouth

STRIPPER

Summer aligned
over pale shoulders
stripping cannibal illusion woman
the wind drifts
over cotton wrinkles
where callous hands ache
tying the legs of moon in knots
around waist
she pounds mutated misery
into motion
into wet concrete
she leaves her hand print

THE SUNRISE ON HER LIPS

Fluttering fires disappear
I stare at her
eating blinks
with my eyes

her hands cover vampire dreams
her fingers trace violence to a trance
her body orchestrates nightmares
my body haunted/distant

THIS RIVER

Soft spoken river
tall handsome river
that comes down to us

listen to the river
rumbling through Okanagan
carrying the voices of our people

over the white water
over white/water
power of words/sounds

carrying the hearts
of the people
into the next generation

IN THESE ROLES

I watch your fading/light
all the way
into the long lasting night

in these roles
we cannot change
fading memories

I needed your bones
I needed your laughter
nightmares/walking out

I roll it all out
and now
only the darkness responds

in these roles
you whisper/*dawn*
to the night/one lonely kiss

I spilled some whiskey on your grave
and watched it seep hard
through the church yard dirt

MAKING YOU STAY

I could trap you in a net
but you would only tear it up

I could build a wall
but you would only break it down and make it fall

I could build a gate
but your beams would still shine through

tell me how can I harness you?
would it take an army of thousands to make you stay?

or just a word and a tear
to take your wings and keep you here

GRANDFATHER/STONES

We left our lives
behind
seen/done/remembered

one winter
we gathered together a sacred circle
listening to the grandfather/stones

with the smell of
sweetgrass
all around us

healing

DO YOU REMEMBER THESE SCARS?

I am lonesome for the snow
Do you remember these scars on my body?
Do you remember the rain like nails pounding into the earth?

said you needed me to hold sometimes
said it used to snow in November
walked with the wind blowing against you

with the moon's jaundiced eye on your breasts
waited at the crossing
for the trains

we waited for the trains
boxcars of rage
dark woman

you are the earth
standing like a star
dripping all over the world

SHIVER

Now violence begins
the night is falling
and the cops there is no one to hear/no one here
our reservation with its long dark winters crawling
over pink and green houses

the women are in church singing
the girls are screaming at their brothers to stop/STOP
the nightmare begins here on our reservation
the women are falling
the men are drinking

no one is fishing
no one is working
the church is full
and our daughters are drowning
one by one

the Whiteman nightmare comes
crawling out of the muskeg
their hearts bound to their bones
and even the darkness begins to shiver
over pink and green houses

HIGH UP VOICES

It was here
God put
the Indians

here
I gnaw off
all my limbs

here
painted
misery

BEGIN/AGAIN

There is a dim light
crawling over the ripped open ground

begin again/begin again the night
begin again the falling down

begin again the rising up
begin again/begin again

the mothers/fathers/sons and the brothers
the sisters and the daughters

the shouting/sweating and the tearing of the day
into the night

begin again with one little hand carving
pieces of life from my bones

GETTING A/WAY

We draw a path that
we will take with the ghosts

wily young woman
wily young man

ghosts of spits of gas
were all there really was

the ghosts of our relatives
with kerosene lamp lighted you

and me higher than path to your grandmother's
I thought I would die of laughter

with you by my side
both of us anxious to get a/way

AT HER FATHER'S GRAVE

Horizontal white knuckles
still hold the breath of the dead

the eyes of the dying
no escape/ this grave

voices sweet/ sad and silent
she bleeds

hands/ covered in blood
prayers in her fists

HOME FROM THE HOTEL

One boy
half the night
passing
staggering body
one girl
dragging
staggering body
the summer
sick
all the way to autumn
this route
these sidewalks
come sleep these steps
until morning

THE CROWS TOLD ME SHE WAS COMING

Like the sound of breaking glass
they made me
they broke the silence
through the trees
they told me
through the snow
through the frozen air
she came
she disappeared again
like the sound of
breaking glass

RAINBOW WOMAN'S UNCHAINING

This is where you danced
with the rainbow woman
grandma
this is where my father
danced with her too
I can see her now grandpa
she is dancing with me
spinning me
my bones are rattling
my children are watching
she has made me old
and now
she is holding her hands
out to them

BUILT WITH THE RAIN

With the rain I build
with the rain I build
with the rain I build

pictures
of
you

PAVEMENT SONG

Hello it's me
where are you?
how do I get to you?
I'll only be here
for the duration of the darkness
which is as long as you need me
I'll only be here
until the wheels stop spinning
I've been following these headlights
all of my life
this night is built for
the echoes of lonely travellers
calling out/calling out
from broken bridges
and exhausted concrete
carrying me to
your room of gypsy memories
I am here following
the map of my hands
driving with my eyes closed
into the night
with its electric light saints
pointing out
back to the highway

THE SLAUGHTER HOUSE ANIMALS

I looked at the cows
in the slaughter house
a factory of frenzy
hormones and antibiotics spilling everywhere

killing/ illing/ lling/ ling/ ing/ ng
sound of thousands butchered
became so much noise
so much precise carnage

WITH DEAD RATS AND WORN-OUT WORDS

Stepping off main/street
into the darkness
of the alley

rats eat dead rats
and listen/worn-out words
in my mouth

wrap the moon/light around my body
poetry is born/again
I hear the rats gnawing

A BOX OF PALE POEMS ROTTING ON THE FLOOR

I pour myself a beer
inhale off the foam
swallow Mozart's violin sonatas

your love was carcinogenic to me
violins begin to whisper
I turn it off, fuck'em

this night will be
eaten away
silent

I drink beer
listen to the birds
restless and pale

this night is a box of pale poems
rotting on the floor
carcinogenic hearts

I drink
before the morning
can heal any of us

HE WAS AN AQUA VELVA MAN

I've been alone with myself
pumping shotgun holes into
dead poets and dead whores
Leonard brings me bread
Irving brings me wine
while I crucify poems
that I fathered
in blue
in drugstores
and in the dark

MODERN STATE OF LOVE

From above/across
firestorm over Dresden/violence earth/25 000
mourning the buffalo/drowning 10 000 caribou

boxcar brings
letters of love
all the way from Disneyland

killing 40 000
in one blow
a solid STATE

becoming homesick/sick
coming
home

THIS CONFESSION IS NOT ABOUT LOVE

My confession
is charred like a vampire
caught in the sun
when it dies
I know I have drowned before
in a river built with the rain/ dreaming
taking the world
to the deepness of sleep

WITH WHISPERS TURNING ME TO WATER

With poets drunk and deaf
sear my throat with
smoke/silent
till it soars/leaves
choking out words

half broken time
into wounds
with whispers turning me to water
repleaded with pus
faithful to the currents

DANDELION WINE

The last time we got drunk together
it was dandelion wine
with nothing else
left to run from
except ourselves
all night
we danced with distant stars

INTO THE DARKNESS

The Sally Ann sandwich wagon is stopping at the park
and the homeless attack
like Indians in John Wayne movies

drunks gather at the seven/11 near now
to gnaw on fried chicken
and potato wedges

I am licking up antifreeze
night swallows us whole
we taste no sleep

TRANSFORMATIONS

I gave the first five years of my life
being human

I spent the next fifteen years of my life
being ashamed and not knowing why (halfbreed)

I lived the next ten years of my life
trying to end it

I'll live the rest of my life
trying to remember what it was to be human

ONE

You opened up your veins and said
This is my art gallery, I am lonesome
for something I can cherish
and know the sun is almost gone

can you hear me calling out
calling out to you
with deep wounds
in my hands?

can you hear me
on this rock
from these rising waters
with these chains on my wrists?

I have been dancing
with half of my heart
waiting for the black winter
and snow like ash

I am calling out to you
with the black sky dripping
I want to wrap my arms around you
like a minuteman missile

I want to carry the memories of this *art*
to the asylum
and take half of the broken
earth with me

SKUNK!

A skunk would waddle through the alley way
behind our house at night
after a few weeks I noticed
it was usually Saturday night
I was lucky
I've never seen him
my dog however
was not

RE-INVENTING DESTRUCTION

The wind blows
through the pony's hair
in the carcass of the dog who ate it
they sit atop civilization
rotting
the hooves rattle
the sound carried away
on the wind

WOLVES WONDER INTO CAMP

Oh great hunter
          laying still

his body fused to the snow

the remaining dog team nervous

          and helpless
          begin to mush on

gee!
haw!

the winter night
covers the eye

WHILE OUTSIDE THE TRIPLE/3

The girls
lean forward
against
passenger
doors
money
pass hand to hand
cars
vomit the bodies
back out
on to the street

TROPHY HUNTER

The blood drips into the slush
over shale ice
flesh turns rancid

they portage
moose/heads
through bush

this silent mass
strangling a pale blue sky
hunting the land and killing it

LEAVING A CITY INSIDE YOU

3/inch thick love affair
with one brick wall
gone/gone/gone

concrete arms
hold you
hold up the night

wrap you threaded heart
around the pavement
long

I remember we went walking
with our horses
over the railroad
and the whispers stayed forever

gone/one/ne/e

the horses became wild
ran free
leaving me
beside
railroad

you cannot bend the sunlight
or tilt it
toward me
behind a bri/concrete/k wall

sunlight is trapped
in one straight line
broken
only by shadows

GOD'S WOMAN

We were so young
she says
God
she says
was still creating animals then
and building rivers
he wanted to put the south Saskatchewan
in Greece
but she talked him out of it
and to call dogs/cats
and cats/dogs
everyone talked him out of that one
she says
she says
it's a good thing he has me
to tell him what to do

MEETING YOU AGAIN

I've been sleeping in the rain
and abandoned railroad stations
this you say
is walking on water
this you say
is what keeps dead men alive
this is your imagination
this city is just blue café
after blue café
and will not
wipe away the dust
from these years
in/between us

I SMELL SUMMER ON YOUR MOUTH

I smell summer on your mouth
kiss your winter scars
where the earth was born

dew rolling
down your hills
beneath night sky

your body wraps around me
beckoning me
into your mouth

I exhale
and climb on to
your tongue

WATCHING THE SLOW MURDER

I sit on the porch
sometimes at night
sometimes in the morning
sometimes with *Wild Turkey*

I watch the night fall or the sunlight crawl
out of the sky but always with my dog
my dog snaps at the moths that gather
or lays in the dew

I sit and watch
the city becomes cannibal
slaughtering its inhabitants
with noise

SEE THESE SCARS

These scars
are lies
we tell ourselves
to stay alive

they will
never heal
we remain
unforgiven

we listen
we say
we tire

WITNESS TO A WOMAN IN LABOUR

Woman when I look at you
I see the earth
being born
water breaking
clouds rise at your feet
and fall at your toes
the rain falls
on to your body
the flood
making life again

CREATION

My one whore heart
is in two pieces
one to cover the sky
one to cover the land
over the womb
I burn the flesh of cedars
till their bones
became ash

SLEEPING AT THE BOTTOM

Your poetry can bend the sky
weave webs
between my lips
cleave this light
in my veins

look hard to get under baby
these prisons of my memory
drunk on desire
dripping
from my ancient wound

NEIL STONECHILD AND HIS AFFECTS ON ME

I moved back to Ontario
when Dudley George was killed with one OPP bullet
I was travelling through Alberta
when Connie and Ty Jacobs were killed with one
    RCMP bullet

then you happened and I wasn't around
I thought it was me
I thought I was the cause
what was it?
this thing that haunts us

I am still living
to speak to this monster
that haunts the land
and hunts down Indians

COYOTE'S TIME

When we sing
we go back to the beginning
before the earth and light were born
we go to the arch
before the Whiteman came
before the serpent's sorrow
flooded the rivers
and the world cried
before God
with these chants
from our mouths
carrying these white bones
to the time
before the mountains moved
with this song
we sing again creation

CRAZY WHITEGIRL YET SLEEPING

The morning drops dew on your body
the tall wild grasses
painted on your skin

I wish I could speak to you
like mountains and rivers
lying naked in the wind

it's callous voice
it's wild heart dances across my tongue
while the night grows old

DANCING BACK THE SACRED

I am exhausted
jingle dress dancer
of being followed in the pharmacy
of the searches at the border
the stares by the police
of the questions about my "breed"
of being brown
in a Whiteman's world
your feet are aching
and falling hard to the ground
and giving way
a healing
Eagle whistle blowing
bring Mikinauk
with his strong medicine
bring my ancestors
jingle dress dancer
bring Makwa too
my good cousin
wake from your long slumber
Thunderbirds
flying over the world
nesting high up mountains
and Mishipisu
swimming up
from the underwater currents
we dance
we bring you back
to this world
to this foreign thing

Mikinauk - Turtle
Makwa - Bear
Mishipisu - Underwater serpent

TO BUY YOU FLOWERS

Me and the dog
going to buy you flowers
from the front porch
we can hear chains
over concrete
we can see walls
between brown people
and white people
I climb over the corpses left on
barbwire fences
vultures and ravens tear into
the rancid flesh
the dog digs beneath them
we go by the shops
every broken window
beckons its wares
broken washers
busted dryers
and rusted-out cars
we arrive at the flower shop
and the dog waits outside
all the flowers are withered
I pick some wilted daffodils
retrieve the dog and
we make our way home again
blood dripping from our bodies

WHO IN THE HELL CAN WRITE AT HOME?

With the cat and dog fighting
and the boy hollering
and the teevee blaring
dishes piling up
laundry piling up
the phone ringing
the doorbell singing
now the cat is on the table
and the dog is at my lap
someone is still at the door
tap tap tap
now my old lady's coming in
Where's my supper been?
the teevee is still on
and the cat and dog are gone
the laundry piling up
dishes piling up
WHO IN THE HELL CAN WRITE AT HOME?

AFTER OUR MARRIAGE ENDED

I licked every flower and every thorn
I didn't know which was sweeter
the petals or the bleeding
the wind on my hands
before you buried me
in your father's lonely tomb
with his body slowing
turning into dust
here I am lonely
for the light and natural light
in this tomb
the flowers crumbled
and turned black

ONE WASTEFUL DESIRE

My mouth
has only these desires
to suck on your barbed fences
freezing to your rusted wire

my eyes
are watching you
when they close
they cover miles

your whispers
sometimes sweet
sometimes bitter like urine
on my tongue

follow your
bloody footprints
while my arms are chained
to your waist

Coming into Penticton

The heat crawled into the car and
hung inside making it stale
a tiny breeze mixed in with raw sewage and
I sifted it through my nostrils
before the heat could smother it too

the light turned red
the exhaust of motor homes
and pick-up trucks choked everyone
we were all lynched
by the hot poison

the town was the same
as any town we had passed before
it was uniform confined to pavement and glass
all in square boxes
all in stone

the inhabitants
were like statues in stone houses
stone hearts
frozen eyes
with stone below and stone above

we drove back up the mountain
where stone was covered with trees and snow
I looked down at the town
and it stood still
like stone

A MOTHER IS TO LOVE

Two children never share the same mother
one is loved less and one is loved more

this is true
this is survival
this is instinct

mothers lie to their less loved children
tell them they are stronger and need lees love
It is the same, just different

mothers lie because they have to
children believe because they want to

HOME IN THE RAIN

I get to the shop at 5/thirty
and wait along with about thirty other men
the clouds are gathering
Beer clouds, ha?
the right hands huddle near the foremen
their hopes are turned to the clouds
we wait for the supervisor
to make up his fucking mind
Is it gonna rain boss?
Are we going out?
he watches the radar screen
on the weather network
the men wait, smoke in the parking lot
sip coffee, some sip beer in their trucks
hurry up and wait
the foremen head out to their jobs
taking their right hands with them
the rest of us wait
until it starts raining
the kettle men will go home
the labourers will go home
the roofers will go home
in the rain

MY LOVE/BUTTER/FLIES

My love for you is vicious
a sin that is hidden
I vomit
all over it
wrapping it reluctantly
in the blood
of a thousand pale yellow flowers

JIM I-VI

I.

We drank that night, that last night with your giant cans of *Fosters,* I drank all my beer and then I helped myself to yours, because I was a greedy bastard. We talked about Indians and cowboys, because that's what we liked to talk about, that past. We laughed because we liked to laugh, and that's why we drank together.

II.

I remember some woman, she was a tiny woman, her body tight against mine. Her husband came over, and begged her to come home, said the kids wouldn't stop crying. I phoned them a cab and they left. You looked at me, gave me a beer and we talked until dawn.

III.

I remember when you asked me to go and get your boy up in Saskatchewan, in the middle of winter, I rode up there in three days and drank white vodka and yellow beer. I didn't have the boy, I was lost that winter with Chipewyan girls dragging me through the snow, the boys out for blood, but I made it out of P.A. with your boy and the north wind following.

IV.

I saw you hitchhiking to see your boy in the city, the crazy one. I wanted you to be my best man at my wedding and you said you would when you get back. You took your lunch pail, it's easier to get rides if they think you're going to work.

V.

My dad came over two nights later, said you had died, fallen down some stairs, drinking beer. I'd carry your coffin three days later and put it in the ground that November, before it froze. They sent your boy back up to Saskatchewan.

VI.

I drank some rye that winter and it tasted like water. I was silent, drank some more and then I followed the sound of the lake freezing and waited for spring.

I AM THE SUICIDE

I am the suicide
of your dreams
the poet you have forgotten

I am the poem
that shoots Zapatista rebels
in the Chiapas
baptizes Titus[1]
in the bloody jungles
of France

this poet was
written in Panmunjeom[2]
in 1953
and buried alive
with Thomas Scott[3]

this poet was
murdered at Jackson state[4]
and suspended in Quebec[5]

this is the poet
that assassinated Park Chung-hee[6]
and voted for Salvador Allende[7]
and first sold in 1510[8]
and was burned alive in Bhopal[9]

I am the bastard
you're forgotten poet

[1] Titus Flavius Vespasianus, destroyer of the Temple of Jerusalem.

[2] Place where the Korean War ceasefire was signed.

[3] Sentenced to death by the Louis Riel provisional government, precipitating the Riel rebellion.

[4] Jackson State University, two protesters were shot and killed by police in 1970, both were black.

[5] Ref. to October Crisis in Québec in 1970.

[6] Dictator of South Korea, 1961-79.

[7] Marxist-socialist president of Chile, 1970-73, overthrown in a coup with CIA involvement.

[8] King Ferdinand authorizes shipment of Africans to Santo Domingo, thus beginning systematic slavery into the New World.

[9] Ref. to the Bhopal disaster in 1984, est. 25,000 died in a Union Carbide Ltd. gas leak.

ACKNOWLEDGMENTS

Some of these poems have previously appeared in various poetry magazines in print and online, including *Dalhousie Review, Urban Graffiti, Fresh (New Zealand), Saravati (England), Istanbul Literary Review (Turkey), Island (Australia), The New Writer (England),* and *The Blue Collar Review (USA)*. My many thanks to the editors and publishers of these periodicals.